# Gluten free
## Bread · Muffins · Slices · Cakes **baking**

C000142210

Over the past few years we have had many, many requests for a book on gluten free baking – so here it is!

Initially we were a little apprehensive about the prospect. While we had dabbled with some gluten free muffin recipes a few years ago, and were really pleased with some bread recipes we developed last year, we weren't at all sure how we would go with a whole book.

As it turns out, we needn't have worried too much. There were a few hiccups along the way (some recipes we thought would work no problem, didn't, while others we weren't so sure about turned out really well!). Once we 'got the hang of things' we were really impressed by how well our recipes turned out, and the range we were able to come up with.

Some of these recipes are gluten free adaptations of our traditional favourites while for others we started from scratch. Not surprisingly, sometimes the texture of the gluten free version is a little bit different to its conventional cousin (often it is a bit lighter), but we feel these are pretty small changes, and sometime it is even for the better! We think in the end there should be something to keep almost anyone happy.

If you, or someone you cook for is on a gluten free diet, we're sure you'll enjoy this book!

Happy Baking
**Simon & Alison Holst**

## Fundamentals of Gluten Free Baking

Gluten is a protein (or rather a set of proteins) found in wheat (including kamut and spelt) and barley, rye and triticale. Oats don't actually contain gluten, but they do contain a similar protein and/or because of the risk of cross contamination with other grains, they are also usually avoided by those on strict gluten free diets.

While gluten actually makes up a relatively small proportion (usually 8–14%) of wheat flour (compared with 65–75% starch), unfortunately for the gluten free baker, gluten has some almost unique physical properties. When gluten proteins are mixed with water (as in a dough or batter), the molecules interact with one another to form a matrix which has both fluid and elastic characteristics. The elastic nature of these doughs allows them to trap little bubbles of gas (released by yeast or baking powder) which expand during cooking and create a light texture.

The trick then to creating gluten free baked products similar to their conventional (gluten containing) cousins, is to somehow create an elastic mixture.

There are two major ways to do this (which are often used in combination). Eggs, or particularly egg whites can be beaten to a foam that will to some extent hold gas a bit like gluten. The other alternative is to use vegetable gums like guar or xanthan gums. These gums are made of carbohydrates that will hold many, many times their own volume of water. The powdered gums mix with cold water to form thick, sticky gels that again convey a slight elasticity to batters or doughs.

The starchy component of wheat flour can be replaced with maize cornflour, rice flour and/or tapioca flour. These are made from corn, rice and cassava respectively, all of which are gluten free. While in theory any one could be used in place of wheat starch, they do all have slightly different properties and we find we get the best results when they are used in combination. Maize cornflour (and sometime rice flour) can be found at the supermarket. Tapioca flour (or starch) and rice flour can be found in healthfood shops, stores specialising in bulk food, or stores specialising in Asian foods.

While wheat starch (cornflour) it is being removed from more and more mainstream baking ingredients, there are still some products that you should be careful about if on a strict gluten free diet. Make sure you select a gluten free baking powder, likewise icing sugar contains a small amount of added starch, make sure you buy one that is gluten free. Custard powder is also largely starch based; check the label before you buy.

## Baking Basics

When you bake, especially if you want good results each time, you need to be precise and measure (or weigh) the ingredients carefully.

The ingredients in these recipes have been measured rather than weighed, and the quantities given in level cup and spoon measures. We have used standard, metric measuring cups for all the cup measures given. A standard metric measuring cup holds 250 millilitres (quarter of a litre).

A set of "single capacity" measuring cups will

enable you to measure all your dry ingredients quickly and easily. Use a set which has a one cup, half cup and quarter cup measure.

All the dry ingredients you measure in these cups should come right up to the top of the measure, but should not be heaped up in it. The only ingredient which should be packed into a cup is brown sugar. Put it in so that it keeps its shape when turned out, like a sand castle.

Flour (or starch) measurements are especially important when you are baking, since too much will make your mixture stodgy and thick, but too little will make biscuits spread too much, and cause other problems too. When measuring a flour, first stir it lightly in its container, then dip in the measure, lift it out, and level it off with the edge of a knife. Do not shake or bang the measure, since this packs down the flour and means that you will use more than the recipe means you to.

Larger butter quantities have been given by weight. Butter packs have 50g or 100g markings on them. These are accurate, apart from the markings at each end of the pack. Small quantities of butter have been measured by spoons – one tablespoon of butter weighs nearly 15g.

Because household spoons vary so much in size, we always use a set of metric measuring spoons. One tablespoon holds 15ml, and one teaspoon holds 5ml. All the cup and spoon measures in this book are level, unless otherwise stated. Golden syrup is the exception. For convenience we use rounded household spoonfuls for small amounts of this. Dip the spoon in boiling water first, for easier removal.

## Cooking times and temperatures

For cakes, biscuits and other baking, your oven must be heated to the right temperature before the food is put in to bake. Turn on the oven before you do anything else!

We positioned our oven racks just below the middle for everything we cooked, since this allowed the top and bottom to brown in about the same time. Ovens vary however, and you may know, or find out quickly, that in your oven, a slightly higher or lower position is better to get this even colouring.

Ovens with fans cook more quickly than ovens without fans set at the same temperature. For this reason, we have often suggested two temperatures. Where we have not, we found that the temperature variation did not matter, as long as we took our baking out when it was done.

We have found that no two ovens cook in exactly the same way! Because of their variations, you must use some judgment, rather than following exact instructions for cooking times. We often offer a range of times, and as well, tell you what to look for, to judge when your baking is ready. Start looking at your food when it has cooked for three quarters of the suggested time, then look every few minutes, until it is at the right stage. If you have cooked something and found that it was cooked before it browned attractively, turn the oven 5° higher next time. If it browns before it is cooked in the centre, lower the temperature by the same amount next time you make it.

Cooling on racks produces better results than cooling in the baking tin or on the tray.

# Cheese Scones

These aren't as solid as a traditional scone, but they're quick and simple to make (like the traditional version), and they taste delicious – a winning combination.

**For 10–12 scones:**

1 cup rice flour

1 cup tapioca flour

4 tsp baking powder

1 tsp guar gum

½ tsp salt

75g cold butter, cubed

1 cup grated cheese

1 cup milk

A little extra grated cheese to decorate, optional

1. Preheat the oven to 200°C.

2. Sift the flours, baking powder, guar gum and salt into a food processor. Add the cold cubed butter and process in short bursts until the mixture looks like fine crumbs.

3. Add the cheese and process briefly, then, with the processor running, gradually add enough of the milk to make a soft dough.

4. Tip the mixture out onto a sheet of baking paper that has been lightly dusted with rice or tapioca flour. Sprinkle a little more of the flour over the dough, then pat it out to make a roughly rectangular shape about 25cm long by 12cm wide and about 2cm thick.

5. Cut the dough into 10–12 roughly evenly sized portions, then arrange these a few centimetres apart on a baking paper or Teflon lined baking sheet. Sprinkle the tops with a little extra grated cheese if desired.

6. Bake at 200°C for 12–14 minutes or until golden brown.

7. Serve warm or cold.

# Pikelets

These aren't quite the same as regular pikelets, but if anything, they're lighter and fluffier, which we think is a good thing!

**For about 20 pikelets:**

½ cup rice flour

½ cup tapioca flour

2 tsp baking powder

½ tsp guar gum

25g butter, melted

1 large (size 7) egg

1 rounded household tablespoon golden syrup

½ cup milk

**1** Sift the dry ingredients into a medium-sized bowl and stir to combine thoroughly.

**2** Whisk the melted butter, egg, golden syrup, and milk together in a small bowl.

**3** Pour the wet mixture into the dry ingredients, then stir well until smooth. The mixture will be runny at first but should thicken if left to stand for a few minutes. If the mixture is too thick to flow when dropped off a spoon, thin with a little extra milk.

**4** Heat a large, preferably non-stick, frypan over a medium to low heat. Wipe the pan with a thin film of oil, then drop dessertspoonfuls of the mixture into the pan. Cook until bubbles begin to break on the upper surface, then turn and cook until golden brown on the second side too. (If the first side is too dark, reduce the heat a little. Repeat with the remaining batter.

**5** Serve with jam and cream.

# Gingerbread

Gingerbread is a good, all-purpose stand by! We like this version because it is really quick and easy to mix, it cooks in 25–30 minutes, and it's easy to have all the ingredients on hand in the pantry.

**For a 25x11cm loaf:**

50g butter

1 household tablespoon golden syrup

½ cup (packed) brown sugar

1 egg

½ cup rice flour

½ cup tapioca flour

1 tsp guar gum

2 tsp ground ginger

1 tsp cinnamon

1 tsp baking soda

½ cup milk

1. Preheat the oven to 180°C.

2. Melt the butter and golden syrup together in a medium-sized pot. Once they are combined, remove from the heat and beat in the sugar and egg.

3. Sift in all the dry ingredients except the baking soda. Dissolve the baking soda in the milk, then add this to the pot and stir until just combined.

4. Line the bottom and sides of a small loaf tin with baking paper, then pour in the fairly thin mixture.

5. Bake at 180°C for 25–30 minutes or until the centre springs back when pressed, and until a toothpick comes out clean.

6. Invert onto a cake cooling rack after five minutes.

7. Serve warm or cool – it always seems particularly good with butter!

# Blueberry Muffins

Somewhere along the line, blueberry muffins seem to have become the 'standard' sweet muffin, so we decided they really ought to be the ideal candidate for a 'gluten free make-over'. These are best served warm from the oven or reheated.

**For 12 medium-sized muffins:**

1 cup brown sugar

½ cup canola oil

2 eggs

1¼ cups plain or fruit flavoured yoghurt or unsweetened yoghurt

1 tsp vanilla essence

¼ tsp salt

1 cup fine cornmeal

1 cup rice flour

3 tsp baking powder

1 tsp cinnamon

1 cup frozen blueberries

1. Preheat the oven to 200°C (190°C fanbake), with the rack just below the middle.

2. Measure the sugar and oil into a food processor, and process until smooth. Add the eggs and process again until the mixture is light and creamy looking.

3. Pour in the yoghurt and vanilla, then sprinkle in the salt. Process until mixed.

4. Measure in the cornmeal, rice flour, baking powder and cinnamon, then process in short bursts until there are no lumps. Remove the processor blade, then add the blueberries and stir by hand just enough to mix them evenly through.

5. Thoroughly non-stick spray 12 regular muffin pans, then divide the mixture evenly between them using two large spoons.

6. Bake for 12–15 minutes or until golden brown. Remove from the oven and leave to stand for 3–4 minutes before removing from the pans.

7. Best enjoyed warm from the oven or reheated.

# Double Chocolate Muffins

These wheat-free muffins make a treat for anybody who cannot eat a chocolate cake made with flour, and will be enjoyed by everyone in the family. They can be "dressed up" for a party, too.

**For 12 medium-sized muffins:**

1 cup rice flour

¼ cup cocoa powder

½ tsp baking soda

½ tsp salt

1 cup caster sugar

2 eggs, separated

1 cup plain or fruit flavoured yoghurt

½ cup chocolate chips

1. Preheat the oven to 200°C (190°C fanbake), with the rack just below the middle.

2. Sift the rice flour, cocoa, baking soda and salt and half of the sugar into a large bowl.

3. Separate the eggs, putting the whites into a large clean glass or metal bowl, and mixing the yolks with the yoghurt in another container.

4. Using an electric (or hand) beater, beat the egg whites until their peaks turn over when the beater is lifted from them, then add the remaining sugar and continue to beat until they will again form peaks that turn over.

5. Stir the egg yolk and yoghurt mixture into the dry ingredients then fold in a third of the beaten egg whites. Gently fold in the remaining egg whites and the chocolate chips. This should make a very soft, light batter.

6. Spoon the batter into 12 well sprayed or oiled muffin pans and bake at 200°C for 12–15 minutes until firm when pressed in the centre.

7. Serve warm or cold. Cut out centres, fill with whipped cream for "fairy cakes" for wheat-free diets, if desired.

# Jalapeno, Coriander & Corn Muffins

These muffins, made without wheat flour, have a slightly different texture to 'regular' muffins, but are interesting and well-flavoured. They disappear remarkably fast – often before cooling so the difference is obviously not a worry.

**For 12 medium-sized muffins:**

2 cups grated tasty cheese

2 cups fine yellow cornmeal*

1 tsp baking soda

2 tsp cream of tartar

¾ tsp salt

1 tsp ground cumin

2 Tbsp chopped fresh coriander leaves

1–2 Tbsp chopped (bottled) Jalapeno pepper, optional

2 large eggs

¾ cup milk

* Use cornmeal which is as finely ground as flour, and which is a soft gold colour

**1** Preheat the oven to 200°C (190°C fanbake), with the rack just below the middle.

**2** Measure the grated cheese and cornmeal into a large bowl. Sift in the baking soda, cream of tartar, salt and ground cumin. Toss well to combine, then add finely chopped coriander leaves and Jalapeno peppers, using the larger amount for spicier muffins.

**3** Whisk the eggs and milk together until lightly coloured and frothy on top. Add this immediately to the dry ingredients and mix until evenly combined.

**4** Spoon into 12 non-stick sprayed muffin pans then sprinkle with a little paprika and bake at 200°C for about 12 minutes (until firm when pressed in the centre and lightly browned).

**5** Serve warm or reheated.

# Pistachio Macaroons

**Macaroons are fashionable at the moment – and by happy chance they're also gluten free!**

### For 30–40 'halves':

2 large or 3 small egg whites

pinch of cream of tartar

¼ cup caster sugar

100g shelled pistachios, ground finely

1 cup lightly packed icing sugar

### Ganache:

125g white chocolate

2 Tbsp cream

1 Tbsp orange blossom water (optional)

**1** Place the egg whites in a large clean bowl. Add a pinch of cream of tartar, then beat until they form soft peaks. Sprinkle in the caster sugar, then beat again until the mixture forms stiff peaks.

**2** While the whites beat, grind the pistachios very finely in a blender or food processor. Sift the ground nuts and icing sugar together into a bowl.

**3** Sift the dry mixture (again!) into the egg whites, then fold the mixture together. Getting the texture of the mixture right at this stage will determine the final shape of the biscuits – the more you fold, the more liquid the mixture will become; fold until it just begins to flow.

**4** Bake at 150°C for 20–25 minutes. Leave to cool on the trays for a few minutes, then lift off onto racks to cool completely.

**5** To make the ganache, place the chocolate in a small bowl with the cream (and orange blossom water if using). Heat by microwaving at 50% (Medium) power for 60–90 seconds stirring every 30 seconds, or by placing the bowl over a pot of simmering water. Stir until smooth then cool until thick enough to spread.

**6** Sandwich the biscuit halves together with about a teaspoon of the ganache, then store in an airtight container.

# Chocolate Chip Cookies

These delicious cookies look big and chunky, but actually have a surprisingly light texture.

**For 24–36 cookies:**

200g softened butter

1 cup brown sugar

2 large eggs

2 tsp vanilla essence

1 cup rice flour

1 cup tapioca flour

3 tsp baking powder

1 tsp guar gum

1 cup chocolate chips

½ cup chopped walnuts, optional

**1** Preheat the oven to 180°C.

**2** Beat the butter and sugar with an electric mixer until light and fluffy. Add the eggs and vanilla and beat briefly to combine.

**3** Sift in the flours, baking powder and guar gum, then beat to combine – the mixture may look very dry initially, but should come together to form a soft dough after a minute or so. Add the chocolate chips and chopped walnuts (if using) and stir these through the mixture.

**4** Line two baking sheets with baking paper or Teflon liners. Drop heaped tablespoonfuls of the mixture onto the baking sheets, leaving at least 5cm for spreading between each.

**5** Place one tray at a time in the middle of the oven. Bake at 180°C for 10–12 minutes or until the cookies just begin to darken around the edges.

**6** Allow to cool on the trays for a few minutes before removing and cooling completely on a rack. Transfer to an airtight container for storage.

# Double Chocolate & Raspberry Cookies

**These large cookies make a perfect decadent treat!**

### For about 20 cookies:

125g butter, softened

1 cup brown sugar

1 large (size 7) egg

¾ cup tapioca flour

½ cup rice flour

1 tsp baking powder

¼ cup cocoa powder

90–100g dark chocolate, roughly chopped

½ cup (about 75g) frozen raspberries

1. Preheat the oven to 180°C.

2. Measure the softened butter and sugar into a large bowl. Add the egg, then beat the mixture until pale and creamy.

3. Sift in the dry ingredients, then stir to combine. Add the roughly chopped chocolate and the frozen raspberries. Stir again until evenly combined.

4. Using dessertspoons or an icecream scoop, drop spoonfuls of the mixture onto baking paper or Teflon lined baking trays leaving at least 5cm between them for spreading.

5. Place one tray in the middle of the oven and bake for 12–15 minutes at 180°C until the cookies are just beginning to change colour around the edge.

6. Remove from the oven and allow to cool on the tray for a few minutes before transferring to a rack to cool completely.

# Belgian Biscuits

The texture of these biscuits isn't quite the same as their 'regular' cousins, but they have the same spicy flavour and spread a deliciously enticing smell through the house as they bake.

## For about 30 biscuits (60 halves):

### Biscuits:

1 cup brown sugar, packed

200g soft butter

1 large egg

1 tsp cinnamon

2 tsp mixed spice

4 tsp baking powder

1 cup rice flour

1 cup tapioca flour

¼–½ cup raspberry jam to fill

### Icing:

1 cup sifted icing sugar

1 Tbsp soft butter

about 1½ Tbsp lemon juice or water

red jelly crystals (or coloured sugar)

1. To make the biscuits, measure the brown sugar, softened butter and egg into a food processor. Process until creamy looking, then sift in all the dry ingredients. Process again (scrape down the sides if required) until the mixture begins to come together in clumps.

2. Divide the dough in half. Transfer the first half to a square of cling film and pat it out to form a cylinder about 4cm thick, then roll it in the cling film. Repeat with the second half of the dough. Refrigerate the cylinders until firm (about 2 hours).

3. Preheat the oven to 180°C.

4. Working one at a time, unwrap the cylinders, then cut the dough into 5mm slices. Arrange the slices a few centimeters apart on baking paper-lined baking sheets.

5. Bake one tray at time for 8–9 minutes or until the edges of the biscuits just begin to colour. Remove the tray from the oven and cool for a few minutes before lifting onto a rack to cool completely.

6. Sandwich the halves together with ½–1 teaspoon of jam.

7. To ice, mix icing sugar, butter and enough lemon juice or water to make a fairly soft icing. Spread a little onto the top of each sandwiched biscuit. Sprinkle a few red jelly crystals on the icing if desired.

# Louise Cake

This is a long-time family favourite – Simon fondly remembers his grandmother always seeming to have some stashed away. Here's our gluten free version which we think stacks up very favourably and it's not hard to make.

## Base:

100g softened butter

½ cup sugar

2 (large) egg yolks

1 tsp vanilla essence

1 cup rice flour

½ cup tapioca flour

½ cup maize cornflour

2 tsp baking powder

2 Tbsp water

## Filling:

½ cup good quality raspberry jam

## Topping:

2 large egg whites

1 tsp vanilla essence

½ cup sugar

¾ cup coconut shreds

**1** Preheat oven to 160°C (150°C if using fan bake), with the rack just below the middle. Line the bottom and sides of an 18x28cm tin with baking paper.

**2** For base, put the softened butter and sugar in a food processor or large bowl. Separate two eggs, adding the yolks to this mixture (and put the whites in a clean medium-sized bowl ready to use for the topping). Add the vanilla, and mix to combine, then add the flours and mix again. Sprinkle in the water and process again until evenly crumbly. Tip crumbly mixture into prepared pan and press down evenly. Bake for 15 minutes.

**3** For topping, beat the egg whites and vanilla until frothy, then add the sugar and beat until the tips of peaks turn over when the beater is lifted from them. Then fold ½ cup of the coconut evenly through the meringue.

**4** For filling, spread the jam over the warm base.

**5** Put the meringue in spoonfuls on top, then spread evenly with a knife. Sprinkle with the remaining coconut. Bake for about 15 minutes or until the meringue feels crisp and is evenly and lightly coloured.

**6** Cool completely before cutting into pieces of the desired size.

**7** Serve with tea or coffee. Store preferably one layer deep in a cool place, with lid slightly ajar.

# Chocolate Caramel Bars

This is the perfect sweet treat to enjoy with a cup of tea or coffee, or perhaps to include as a little something special in a lunchbox.

## Base:

125g cold cubed butter

¼ cup caster sugar

½ cup rice flour

½ cup tapioca flour

¼ cup cocoa powder

1 Tbsp water

## Filling:

100g butter

½ a 400g can sweetened condensed milk

½ cup golden syrup

## Icing:

1 Tbsp cocoa

1½ Tbsp boiling water

2 tsp soft butter

¼ tsp vanilla

1 cup icing sugar

1. Preheat oven to 170°C (160°C fanbake), with the rack just below the middle. Line an 18x28cm tin with baking paper.

2. For base, measure the cold cubed butter and sugar into a food processor, then sift in the flours and cocoa powder and process well. Drizzle in the water and process until the mixture looks like fine crumbs. Press the crumbs into the prepared tin. Bake for 8–10 minutes or until the centre is firm.

3. For filling, measure butter, condensed milk and golden syrup into a pot. Bring to the boil over medium heat, stirring all the time, then reduce heat and cook for 10 minutes, stirring often, until the mixture is a deep golden colour, and a drop of it forms a soft ball in cold water.

4. Remove from heat and pour over cooked base straight away, smoothing it out if necessary. Leave to cool before icing.

5. For icing, pour boiling water on cocoa in a small bowl. Beat in butter, vanilla and sifted icing sugar, adding more water if necessary, to make icing soft enough to spread easily over the caramel.

6. Leave uncovered for at least two hours before cutting into bars.

7. Serve with tea or coffee, or as an after dinner treat.

# Lemon Square

This square has a delicious lemon flavoured custard topping and always disappears very fast.

## Base:

1 cup tapioca flour

1 cup rice flour

½ cup icing sugar

125g cold butter

2 Tbsp water

## Topping:

1½ cups sugar

thinly peeled rind of
½ lemon

3 large eggs

¼ cup lemon juice

¼ cup custard powder
flour

½ tsp baking powder

**1** Preheat oven to 160°C (150°C fanbake), with the rack just below the middle. Press a large piece of baking paper into an 18–28cm tin, folding the paper so it covers the bottom and all sides. Do not cut the paper at the corners, or filling will run underneath.

**2** For base, measure the flours, icing sugar and cubed butter into a food processor. Process until butter is chopped finely through dry ingredients. With the processor running, drizzle in the water. Tip mixture into the lined pan and press down firmly and evenly. Bake for 15–20 minutes until firm and just beginning to brown lightly.

**3** For topping, put the sugar in the dry, unwashed food processor with the rind peeled from half the lemon (use a potato peeler for this). Process until the rind is very finely chopped through the sugar, then add the eggs, lemon juice and custard powder, and process until smooth.

**4** Pour over partly cooked base, then bake for about 30 minutes longer, or until top is lightly browned and centre does not wobble when pan is jiggled.

**5** When quite cold, cut into squares or fingers of desired size, by pressing a heavy, lightly oiled knife straight down through the topping and base.

**6** Dust with icing sugar, then serve cut in larger pieces for dessert, with Greek-style yoghurt or lightly whipped cream.

**7** Serve small pieces with tea or coffee at any time of day. Store lightly covered, up to 3 or 4 days.

# Chocolate Brownie

The term 'brownie' seems to encompass quite a range of products – from dense and fudgy to light and cakey. This one is dense and moist, but still has a fine cakey texture.

**For an 18x28cm brownie:**

100g butter

90–100g dark chocolate, chopped

1 cup sugar

3 large (size 7) eggs

2 tsp vanilla essence

½ cup tapioca flour

½ cup rice flour

¼ cup cocoa powder

1 tsp guar gum

½ tsp baking soda

¼ tsp salt

½ cup chopped walnuts, optional

1. Preheat the oven to 180°C.

2. Cut the butter into 3–4 pieces and place in a medium-sized pot along with the chopped chocolate. Heat over a medium-low heat, stirring frequently, until the chocolate has just melted.

3. Remove the pot from the heat and stir in the sugar, then break in the eggs and add the vanilla essence and stir until smooth and evenly combined. Sift in flours, cocoa powder, guar gum, baking soda and salt then stir until well combined. Fold in the walnuts, if using.

4. Line an 18x28cm brownie pan with baking paper, then pour in the brownie mixture.

5. Bake in the middle of the oven for 25–30 minutes or until a skewer poked in the centre comes out clean.

6. Remove from the oven and allow to cool in the pan for about 5 minutes before removing from the pan and cooling on a rack.

7. Cut as desired, then dust with icing sugar before serving.

# Ginger Crunch

Ginger Crunch is another perennial family favourite; even though it seems to have been around forever, it is still popular. Make it yourself, or better still, teach your kids how to make it for themselves – there are a couple of steps, they're not really very complicated.

## Base:

125g butter

¼ cup sugar

1 tsp baking powder

½ cup rice flour

½ cup tapioca flour

1 tsp ground ginger

1 Tbsp cold water

## Icing:

3 Tbsp butter

3 tsp ground ginger

3 rounded household Tbsp golden syrup

4 tsp water

3 cups icing sugar

**1** Preheat oven to 180°C (170°C fanbake), with the rack just below the middle.

**2** Line the sides and bottom of a pan about 18x28cm with baking paper, allowing enough extra paper on the sides for lifting the cooked slice out, or thoroughly non-stick spray a 23cm square loose bottomed pan.

**3** For base, cut the cold butter into nine cubes, then process in brief bursts with remaining base ingredients, until the mixture is the texture of coarse breadcrumbs. If mixing by hand, warm butter until soft, mix it with the sugar, and then stir in the sieved dry ingredients.

**4** Spread the crumbly mixture into the pan and press it down firmly and evenly. Bake for about 10 minutes or until evenly and lightly browned. It will still feel soft while it is hot. While the base cooks make the icing, since the base should be iced while hot.

**5** For icing, measure the butter, ginger, golden syrup and water into a small pot or microwave bowl. Heat, without boiling, until melted. Remove from the heat, sift in the icing sugar, and beat until smooth. As soon as the base is cooked, remove it from the oven. Pour the warm icing onto the hot base and spread carefully so it covers the base evenly. Sprinkle with chopped nuts if desired, then leave the square to cool and set, marking it into pieces while still warm. Do not remove from the pan until it has cooled completely.

# Orange Cake

This is a good 'everyday' cake. It's simple (and delicious) enough to be eaten 'as is', but when the need (or whim) arises it can also be dressed up by icing it, or the mixture also makes good cupcakes.

**For a 21cm ring cake (or about 12 cupcakes):**

1 cup sugar

125g butter

3 large eggs

1 large or two small oranges

1 cup tapioca flour

¾ cup rice flour

2 tsp baking powder

1 tsp guar gum

water

1 Tbsp lemon juice

**1** Preheat oven to 180°C (170°C fanbake), with the rack just below the middle. Line a (7–8 cup capacity) 21cm ring pan with baking paper or a Teflon liner and coat well with non-stick spray.

**2** Thinly peel the orange with a vegetable peeler. Put the peel in a food processor with the sugar and process until finely chopped. Add the softened (but not melted) butter and the eggs, and process until thoroughly mixed. Measure in the flours, then add the juice from the orange/s made up to ½ cup with water, and the lemon juice. Process briefly, just enough to mix, then spoon into the prepared ring pan.

**3** Bake for 35–50 minutes, until skewer in the middle comes out clean. Leave to stand for 5–10 minutes, then remove from the pan. Invert on a rack, and dust generously with icing sugar, or when cool, spread with orange or lemon icing (page 22).

**4** For cupcakes: divide the mixture between 12 (or so) paper lined muffin cups, filling each cup about two thirds full. Bake at 180°C for 10–12 minutes or until firm when pressed lightly in the centre.

**5** When cool, ice with lemon icing (page 22), if desired.

# Chocolate Cake

This makes a large cake, perfect for a party or special occasion, or, when you just feel like a delicious moist chocolate cake! If you want something particularly decadent, ice it with ganache (below) or use your favourite icing.

## For a 23cm cake:

3 large (size 7) eggs, separated

¼ tsp cream of tartar

½ cup oil

1 cup plain unsweetened yoghurt

2 tsp vanilla

1½ cups sugar

1 cup rice flour

1 cup tapioca flour

½ cup cocoa powder

1 tsp guar gum

1 tsp baking soda

½ tsp salt

## Ganache icing:

125–150g dark chocolate

¼ cup sour cream

1. Preheat the oven to 180°C.

2. Separate the eggs and place the whites in a large clean bowl. Add the cream of tartar then beat the egg whites until they form stiff peaks.

3. Place the yolks in another bowl or jug, then add the oil, yoghurt, vanilla and sugar then whisk to combine.

4. Sift the dry ingredients into the egg whites, pour the yoghurt-yolk mixture over the dry ingredients, then gently fold everything together until just uniformly mixed.

5. Non-stick spray and/or line a 23cm round tin with baking paper. Pour the batter into the prepared tin and level the top if required.

6. Place the cake in the middle of the oven and bake at 180°C for 40–50 minutes or until a skewer inserted in the middle comes out clean. Remove from the oven and allow to cool for 5–10 minutes before removing from the tin and cooling completely on a rack.

7. To make the icing, gently heat the dark chocolate with ¼ cup sour cream until just melted, stir until smooth and glossy, then leave to cool until thick enough to spread.

8. Leave the cake to stand until the icing is firm, then serve as is or with yoghurt or lightly whipped cream.

# Carrot Cake

A good carrot cake is hard to go past. This one is nice enough to enjoy un-iced (try serving it as a dessert warm from the oven with ice cream on the side). However, if you're willing to make a little extra effort, the icing definitely adds another dimension.

### For a 21cm ring cake:

½ cup canola or other oil

2 large eggs

1 cup brown sugar

½ cup tapioca flour

½ cup potato starch

1 tsp guar gum

1 tsp baking soda

2 tsp baking powder

2 tsp ground cinnamon

1 tsp ground mixed spice

½ tsp salt

¼ cup milk

1–1½ cups (about 180g) grated carrot

½ cup chopped walnuts, optional

1. Preheat the oven to 180°C.

2. Measure the oil into a large bowl, add the eggs and sugar then beat until pale and creamy looking.

3. Sift in the flours, guar gum, baking soda and powder, spices and salt. Add the milk, then stir until evenly mixed. Add the grated carrot and nuts if using and stir until evenly mixed.

4. Non-stick spray a round 21cm ring tin. Pour the batter into the tin, then bake at 180°C for 30–40 minutes or until a skewer poked in the centre comes out clean.

5. Remove the cake from the oven, allow to cool in the tin for a few minutes before turning it out and cooling completely on a rack.

### Cream Cheese Icing:

½ cup cold cream cheese

1 tsp vanilla essence

1–1¼ cups icing sugar

6. To make the icing, combine the cold cream cheese and vanilla essence in a food processor. Sift in the icing sugar (start with the smaller quantity) and process just enough to mix thoroughly.

# Chocolate & Raspberry Roll

The 'conventional' version of this sponge roll has been a stand by in our house for decades, celebrating many birthdays and special occasions.

**For a 22x30cm sponge roll:**

3 large eggs

½ cup sugar

¼ tsp salt

¼ cup tapioca flour

¼ cup maize cornflour

½ tsp guar gum

2 Tbsp cocoa

1 tsp baking powder

1 Tbsp boiling water

Filling, see right

**Variation:** If preferred, cool the sponge flat, then cut it into two or three pieces and layer these, instead of forming a roll.

1 Preheat oven to 230°C (220°C if using fanbake), with the rack just below the middle. Beat the eggs, sugar and salt together in a fairly large bowl, until mixture is thick, creamy and pale. (Use room temperature eggs and don't hurry the beating.) Meantime, line the bottom and sides of a 22x30cm sponge roll tin with a piece of baking paper. Spray with non-stick spray.

2 Sift the dry ingredients into a clean bowl, return mixture to the sieve, and sift it again onto the thick egg mixture. Fold in carefully but thoroughly. Add the boiling water and fold it in too, then spread the thick mixture evenly in the lined tin.

3 Bake for 7–10 minutes or until the centre springs back when pressed lightly. (Take care not to cook longer than necessary or the sponge will shrink.)

4 Moisten (wet it lightly, then wring well) a clean tea towel and lay it on a large board or the bench. When the roll is cooked turn it out of the tin onto the tea towel. Carefully lift off the baking paper, then using the tea towel to help get started, roll the sponge up (in the tea towel) and leave to cool on a rack.

5 **Filling and decorating:** When cooled to room temperature, carefully unroll, spread with raspberry jam, then whipped rum cream. (Beat 1 cup of cream with ¼ cup icing sugar and 1–2 Tbsp rum until thick.) Roll up, starting from a short end, lifting the tea towel to help you.

6 Serve join-side down, as is, or dusted with icing sugar, with chocolate or white chocolate curls for extra decoration, if you like.

# Gluten free White Bread

Although this isn't exactly like a wheat-based bread, we think it's pretty close. The flavour and texture are good and it can be used for sandwiches and/or toast just as you would regular bread.

## For a 750g loaf:

2 tsp instant active yeast

1 cup warm water plus 2 Tbsp extra

3 tsp sugar

1½ tsp salt

3 tsp guar gum

1 large egg plus 1 large egg white

¼ cup skim milk powder

3 Tbsp canola oil

½ cup (65g) chickpea flour

½ cup (65g) tapioca flour

1 cup (140g) rice flour

1 cup (150g) maize cornflour

1 **Bread Machine:** Carefully measure all the ingredients into a 750g capacity bread machine. For the most effective mixing, it is best to add the liquids first.

2 Set to the GLUTEN FREE bread cycle, MEDIUM crust and START.

1 **By Hand:** Measure the yeast, water, sugar and salt into the bowl of a heavy-duty mixer and leave to stand for 5 minutes.

2 Sprinkle in the guar gum (do this gradually to avoid it forming lumps), then add the egg and egg white and the milk powder. Beat on a medium-high speed for 2 minutes until the mixture looks foamy.

3 Add the oil and flours, then mix again at medium speed for 2 minutes, stopping and scraping down the sides of the bowl after about 1 minute.

4 Thoroughly coat the inside of a large loaf tin with non-stick spray, then pour/spoon the batter into it. Spread the batter evenly in the tin and smooth the top with an oiled spatula.

5 Put the tin in a warm place to rise for 50–60 minutes or until the mixture has reached to the top of the tin.

6 Bake at 200°C for 15–20 minutes until golden brown and hollow sounding when tapped. Remove from the oven and cool in the tin for a few minutes before tipping onto a rack to cool completely.

# Gluten free Fruit & Nut Loaf

Nothing beats the smell of a spicy bread baking (well, maybe the smell of it being toasted) – and this is no exception.

## For a 1kg loaf:

2 tsp instant active yeast

1 cup plus 2 Tbsp warm water

2 Tbsp sugar

1½ tsp salt

50g butter, softened

3 tsp guar gum

2 large eggs

¼ cup skim milk powder

½ cup (55g) chickpea flour

1½ cups (190g) tapioca flour

1 cup (150g) maize cornflour

¼ cup brown sugar

2 tsp ground cinnamon

½ tsp ground mixed spice

½ cup each sultanas and walnut pieces

**1** **Bread Machine:** Carefully measure all the ingredients into a 750g capacity bread machine. For the most effective mixing, it is best to add the liquids first.

**2** Set to the GLUTEN FREE bread cycle, MEDIUM crust and START.

**1** **By Hand:** Measure the yeast, water, first measure of sugar, the salt and butter into the bowl of a heavy-duty mixer and leave to stand for 5 minutes.

**2** Sprinkle in the guar gum (do this gradually to avoid it forming lumps), then add the egg and egg white and the milk powder. Beat on a medium-high speed for 2 minutes until the mixture looks foamy.

**3** Add flours, brown sugar, spices, sultanas and nuts, then mix again at medium speed for 2 minutes, stopping and scraping down the sides of the bowl after about 1 minute.

**4** Thoroughly coat the inside of a large loaf tin with non-stick spray, then pour/spoon the batter into it. Spread the batter evenly in the tin and smooth the top with an oiled spatula.

**5** Put the tin in a warm place to rise for 50–60 minutes or until the mixture has reached to top of the tin.

**6** Bake at 200°C for 15–20 minutes until golden brown and hollow sounding when tapped. Remove from the oven and cool in the tin for a few minutes before tipping onto a rack to cool completely.

# Gluten free Ciabatta or Pizza Base

Most gluten free breads are made from a mixture more like a batter than a dough. This is made from a stiffer mixture which can be shaped more like a traditional dough.

## For 1 ciabatta-style loaf or one large pizza base:

½ cup warm water

2 tsp yeast

2 tsp sugar

1 tsp salt

3 tsp guar gum

1 Tbsp canola oil

2 egg whites

1 cup (125g) tapioca starch

1 cup (140g) rice flour

¼ cup skim milk powder

up to ¼ cup warm water

**1** **Bread Machine:** Measure all the ingredients, including the extra water, into the bread machine. Set to the DOUGH cycle and press start. Check the dough after 5 minutes of mixing and scrape any unmixed flour off the sides. Stop the machine 30 minutes after mixing has started and shape and bake as below.

**1** **By Hand:** Measure the warm water, yeast, sugar and salt into the bowl of a heavy-duty mixer. Leave to stand for 5 minutes, then sprinkle in the guar gum and add the egg whites. Beat at medium speed for 2–3 minutes or until the mixture is pale and slightly foamy looking.

**2** Measure in the flours and milk powder, then mix on medium speed until the mixture begins to bind together. Add as much of the extra water as is required to form a cohesive dough, then mix for 2–3 minutes longer.

**Shaping and Baking:** Thoroughly oil your hands, and lightly oil a baking paper-lined baking tray. Tip/scrape the dough from the mixing bowl or bread machine onto the oiled surface. Lightly sprinkle or spray the dough with oil.

**Pizza:** Gently pat out the dough into an oval shape about 25x35cm of about 5–7mm thickness (placing a sheet of baking paper on top of the dough may make this easier). Allow to rise for 5–10 minutes, then top and bake at 200°C for 12–15 minutes.

**Ciabatta Bread:** Pat the dough into a 25–30cm long and 5–6cm thick sausage shaped loaf. Arrange the loaf on the oiled baking sheet then leave to rise in a warm place for about 1 hour. Bake at 200°C until golden brown and hollow sounding when tapped, about 12–15 minutes.

# Index

Published by Hyndman Publishing
PO Box 19, Amberley, North Canterbury

**ISBN:** 1-877382-69-8
**TEXT:** ©Simon & Alison Holst **DESIGN:** Rob Di Leva **PHOTOGRAPHY:** Lindsay Keats **HOME ECONOMISTS:** Simon & Alison Holst

The recipes in this book have been carefully tested by the authors. The publisher and the authors have made every effort to ensure that the instructions are accurate and śafe, but they cannot accept liability for any resulting injury or loss or damage to property, whether direct or consequential.

Because ovens and microwave ovens vary so much, you should take the cooking times suggested in recipes as guides only. The first time you make a recipe, check it at intervals to make sure it is not cooking faster, or more slowly than expected.

Always follow the detailed instructions given by manufacturers of your appliances and equipment, rather than the more general instructions given in these recipes.